ROCK PIANO CHOPS

by Mark Harrison

HAL•LEONARD®
CORPORATION

7777 W. BLUEMOUND RD. P.O. BOX 13819 MILWAUKEE, WI 53213

ISBN 978-1-4584-1395-6

Published by:
Hal Leonard Corporation
7777 W. Bluemound Road
P.O. Box 13819
Milwaukee, WI 13213

In Australia Contact:
Hal Leonard Australia Pty. Ltd.
4 Lentara Court
Cheltenham, Victoria, 3192 Australia
Email: ausadmin@halleonard.com.au

Printed in the U.S.A.

First Edition

Visit Hal Leonard Online at
www.halleonard.com

Contents

Introduction

Welcome to *Rock Piano Chops*. If you really want to jump-start your rock piano technique so you can play convincingly in modern and classic rock styles, then you've come to the right place! This book gives the beginning-to-intermediate player a complete rock piano workout: you'll develop your rhythmic feel, dexterity, hand coordination, and voicing skills as you work through the fun and authentic exercises. Each example is recorded at several tempos, so you can choose the one that's right for you as you play along with the rock rhythm section on the CD.

First you'll get started with the **Chops-Building Exercises**, which will fire up your technique and voicing chops as you "comp" (accompany) on some classic changes. Then your workout will really get into high gear in our **Groove Lab**, where you'll work with straight and swing rhythmic subdivisions while learning four different ways (from simple to more complex) to play over each of the chord progression examples.

Then in **Phrases and Licks Used by the Pros**, we'll check out some key phrases and techniques used by top rock piano players, so that you can incorporate these ideas into your own music. Finally, in the **Etudes** section, we have longer pieces in the style of legendary rock pianists such as Bruce Hornsby, Chuck Leavell (Rolling Stones), and Billy Joel. These pieces will help you use your rock piano technique in a musically and stylistically effective way.

Good luck with developing and using your Rock Piano Chops!

About the CD

On the accompanying CD, you'll find play-along tracks for almost all of the examples in the book, recorded at several tempos. For each track, the rhythm section is on the left channel and the piano is on the right channel. When you want to play along with the band, turn down the right channel to eliminate the recorded piano. When you want to hear the piano part for reference, turn down the left channel to eliminate the rhythm section. This is designed to give you maximum flexibility when practicing. The rhythm section tracks contain bass and drums, plus a selection of other instruments (guitar, synth, organ, and clavinet).

Chapter 1

Rock Piano Chops-Building Exercises

The Straight-eighths Rhythmic Feel

Most rock styles are written in 4/4 time and use patterns based around eighth or 16th notes. Each of these subdivisions can be played **straight** or **swing**, essentially resulting in four main rhythmic feels:

- Straight eighths
- Swing eighths
- Straight 16ths
- Swing 16ths

In this chapter, we will work on chops-building exercises using straight-eighths and straight-16ths feels. Then, in Chapter 2 (Groove Lab), we will incorporate the swing-eighths and swing-16ths feels.

In a straight-eighths feel, each eighth note is of equal length and divides the beat exactly in half, as follows:

TRACK 1

Note the rhythmic counting below the notes. This is how eighth note rhythms are normally counted, with the 1, 2, 3, and 4 falling on the **downbeats**, and the "&s" falling halfway in between, on the **upbeats**. Check out Track 1 on the CD to get comfortable with this rhythm and counting concept. This is our first and most important rock rhythmic subdivision or "feel," used by the majority of rock songs from the 1960s until the present day.

Straight-eighths Chops-Building Exercises

Now we'll get to the first set of "chops-building" exercises, using the straight-eighths rhythmic feel above. The goal of these exercises is to develop technical dexterity and hand coordination, while also learning chord voicings and rhythm patterns that are appropriate and stylistic for today's rock music.

The CD tracks for the exercises in this section are recorded at three different tempos: 65, 95, and 125 beats per minute (bpm). The exercises are repeated twice at each tempo on the CD tracks.

Depending on your playing level, you can start at the slowest CD tempo as needed, before moving on to the faster tempos. Make sure you are comfortable with the voicings and the rhythms shown, when playing at each tempo. You can check against the piano part on the right channel of the CD. You can also practice hands separately as needed, before combining the hands together on each exercise.

On to our first straight-eighths chops-building exercise.

Straight-eighths Exercise #1

TRACK 2
0:00 65 bpm
0:20 95 bpm
0:35 125 bpm

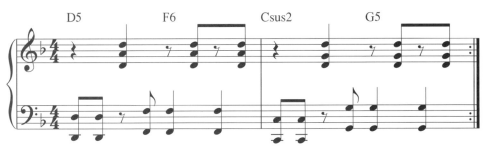

Here, the right hand is repeating the note D in octaves, over the different chords. (Repeating the same note over different changes is called a "pedal point.") Within the right-hand octaves, the notes A and G create internal fourth and fifth intervals, with a hollow and transparent sound suited to modern rock styles. The right-hand voicings use mostly roots, fifths, and ninths on these chords, which also creates a modern sound. The left hand is playing the root of each chord in octaves, again typical for the style.

This groove has an interesting rhythmic alternation between the left- and right-hand parts. In each measure, the right-hand voicing lands on beat 2, which is a **downbeat**, and on the "& of 3" and "& of 4," which are **upbeats**. (See rhythmic counting and text for Track 1.) Meanwhile, the left hand is landing on the remaining downbeats (1, 3, and 4) in between the right-hand voicings, giving the pattern a solid foundation.

Beats 2 and 4 are also referred to as **backbeats** in rock styles, as these are normally where the drummer hits the snare drum. (Check the rhythm track on the left channel as needed.) In rock piano styles, the right hand will often reinforce one or both of these backbeats.

Straight-eighths Exercise #2

TRACK 3
0:00 65 bpm
0:20 95 bpm
0:35 125 bpm

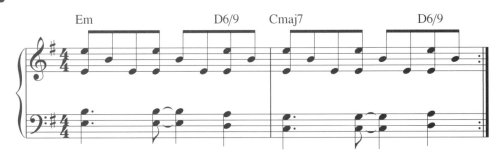

In the right hand, this example takes the tonic and fifth degrees of the key, E and B in the key of E minor, and plays them in an arpeggio (broken chord) style over the chord changes. (Repeating the same arpeggio or melodic line over different changes is called an "ostinato.") This creates a transparent sound and combines with the solid root-fifth voicings in the left hand for an effective modern rock groove.

Rhythmically, there is an emphasis in both hands on beat 1, the "& of 2" (anticipating beat 3), and beat 4. This is one of the most common syncopated rhythms heard across a range of eighth-note rock styles.

Straight-eighths Exercise #3

TRACK 4
0:00 65 bpm
0:20 95 bpm
0:35 125 bpm

This time in the right hand we are using a staple rock piano device I call "minor pentatonic fourth intervals" in my books and classes. These are fourth intervals derived from a minor pentatonic scale, in this case F minor pentatonic, containing the notes F, A♭, B♭, C, and E♭. The above intervals (C-F, E♭-A♭, F-B♭, and so on) can be floated over various chords available in the minor key. Here, the Fm, A♭, B♭, and E♭ chords function as a I, ♭III, IV, and ♭VII respectively in the key of F minor. These are common chords found in many rock songs in minor keys. Meanwhile, the left hand is playing the root of each chord using octaves.

Rhythmically, the left hand is driving the groove by playing on all the eighth-note subdivisions, providing a good foundation below the rhythmic variations in the right hand. Some players will emphasize the downbeats a little more than the upbeats when playing this type of left-hand rock pattern. It's all a matter of taste and preference!

Straight-eighths Exercise #4

TRACK 5
0:00 65 bpm
0:20 95 bpm
0:35 125 bpm

Now we get into blues/rock piano territory with Exercise 4. This groove on a G7 chord uses a number of staple blues piano techniques in the right hand:

- The repeated top note (drone) G and the moving line of D♭ to D come from the G blues scale. This scale in total contains the notes G, B♭, C, C♯ or D♭, D, and F.

- The third intervals C-E and B-D come from the G Mixolydian mode (containing the notes G, A, B, C, D, E, and F). This mode is a C major scale repositioned to start on G, and is a common "scale source" for the G7 chord.

- The B♭-B and D♭-D movements are a "♭3rd to 3rd" and "♭5th to 5th" respectively on the G7 chord, imparting a strong blues flavor.

Meanwhile, the left hand is playing root-fifth and root-sixth intervals with a steady eighth-note rhythm. This is a classic blues/rock pattern derived from boogie-woogie styles. Make sure you play this left-hand pattern with a rock-solid consistency. You can accentuate the downbeats a little more as desired.

Straight-eighths Exercise #5

TRACK 6
0:00 65 bpm
0:20 95 bpm
0:35 125 bpm

This exercise is in a pop/rock style, and alternates between two triads (Eb and F major) in the right hand, over a repeated bass line (bass ostinato) starting on C, in the left hand. Collectively this implies a Cm7 chord, and technically is based on a C Dorian mode, containing the notes C, D, Eb, F, G, A, and Bb. This mode is a Bb major scale repositioned to start on C, and is a common scale source for a Cm7 chord.

This groove gets its energy from the repeated eighth-note bass pattern in the left hand, so make sure you play it in a rhythmically consistent way, to support the triads in the right hand. This type of left-hand pattern sounds better played in a "legato" (smooth and connected) playing style, so try not to leave any gaps between the notes when you play.

Straight-eighths Exercise #6

TRACK 7
0:00 65 bpm
0:20 95 bpm
0:35 125 bpm

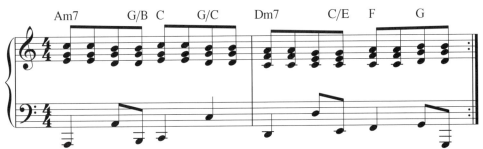

Here is another exercise in a pop/rock style, this time using repeated eighth-note triads in the right hand. Over certain chords we are moving between different triads in the right hand. For example, over the Am7 chord we are moving between the C and G major triads, over the Dm7 chord we are moving between the F and C major triads, and so on. This alternating triad technique is a staple of pop/rock piano styles.

The left-hand pattern is providing important rhythmic and harmonic support to the right-hand triads, playing roots of the chords on all the downbeats, and with some eighth-note pickups leading into beat 3. This is one of the most useful rock left-hand patterns we will encounter! Make sure you play the left-hand pattern in a steady and even way, as a foundation below the right-hand part.

The Straight-16ths Rhythmic Feel

In a straight-16ths feel, each 16th note is of equal length and divides the eighth-note exactly in half—and the beat exactly into quarters, as follows:

TRACK 8

Note the rhythmic counting below the notes. This is how 16th note rhythms are normally counted. In between the beat numbers (1, 2, 3, 4) and the "&s," we now add the "e" on the second 16th note within each beat, and the "a" on the fourth 16th note within each beat. The 16th-note feel is commonly found in the funkier rock styles, often with an emphasis on these extra rhythmic subdivisions that are not available at the eighth-note level.

Straight-Sixteenths Chops-Building Exercises

Next up are the chops-building exercises using the straight-16ths rhythmic feel above. The CD tracks for the exercises in this section are also recorded at three different tempos: 56, 83, and 110 beats per minute. The exercises are repeated twice at each tempo on the CD tracks.

As before, start at the tempo best suited to your playing level, and practice hands separately as needed. On to our first straight-16ths chops-building exercise:

Straight-16ths Exercise #1

TRACK 9
0:00 56 bpm
0:24 83 bpm
0:41 110 bpm

Here, the right hand is playing power chord root-and-fifth voicings on the Dm, F, and G chords. The fourth intervals A-D, C-F, and D-G can also be found in a D minor pentatonic scale. (See Straight-eighths Exercise #3 comments.) Meanwhile, the left hand is playing the root of each chord and using an octave pattern on the Dm and G chords.

Note how the 16th-note rhythms in the right hand combine with the strong downbeat pattern in the left hand, in this funkier rock style. In particular, the energy comes from the right hand landing on the last 16th of beat 1 (the "a of 1") and on the second 16th of beat 4 (the "e of 4"). These subdivisions are not available within the straight-eighths feel we studied earlier. Count this right-hand rhythm aloud with the CD track as needed, to get comfortable with these important 16th-note syncopations!

Straight-16ths Exercise #2

TRACK 10
0:00 56 bpm
0:24 83 bpm
0:41 110 bpm

This time, the right hand is playing a repeated top note of E across the changes, moving from A to B underneath, which results in a series of fourth and fifth intervals. The same right-hand part (containing the notes E, A, and B) is used over both chords, resulting in the chord qualities of Esus and Asus2, respectively.

Note that this groove is rhythmically busier than the preceding Exercise #1. In the first part of each measure, the right hand is using more of the weak 16ths, i.e., the "e" and "a" within the beat. (Review the text accompanying Track 8 as needed.) This creates a more intensely syncopated effect. After playing the root of the chord with the pinky on beat 1 of each measure, the left-hand thumb is repeating the root an octave higher, in a rhythmic conversation with the right-hand part. This is all typical of funk/R&B keyboard styles, and is also used in the funkier rock styles.

Straight-16ths Exercise #3

TRACK 11
0:00 56 bpm
0:24 83 bpm
0:41 110 bpm

In this example, the right hand returns to using triads. These are all basic triads as defined by the chord symbols, except for the E♭ major triad used over the first Cm7 chord. This is an upper structure triad built from the third of the Cm7 chord. This gives us the third, fifth, and seventh of the Cm7 chord in the right hand. Note that we are using inversions to voice lead (move smoothly between) the right-hand triads. The left hand is playing the root of each chord, using an octave pattern, except at the end of measure 2.

Rhythmically, the right hand is landing a 16th note either side of beat 3—that is, on the last 16th of beat 2 (the "a of 2") and on the second 16th of beat 3 (the "e of 3"). This is an important and often-heard rhythmic figure in modern and alternative rock styles. To complement this, the left hand plays the chord roots at the points of chord change, then adds a 16th-note pickup on the last 16th note of beats 1 and 3. This leads effectively into the right-hand chords played on beats 2 and 4, the backbeats.

Straight-16ths Exercise #4

TRACK 12
0:00 56 bpm
0:24 83 bpm
0:41 110 bpm

This busier, more syncopated example is reminiscent of several dance-pop classics. Harmonically, the structure is similar to Straight-eighths Exercise #5, as we are alternating between two triads (F and G major) over the same root (G in this case). The F/G creates a suspended dominant chord: the F triad can be thought of as being built from the seventh of this chord. Alternating between the two chords, F/G and G, implies a G7 chord overall, and is all contained within a G Mixolydian mode. (See Straight-eighths Exercise #4 comments.)

Rhythmically, the right hand is playing an interesting figure: from the second 16th of beat 1 (the "e of 1") onward, each measure is divided up into three-quarters-of-a-beat increments. For example, in the first measure the F major triad on beat 2 is three-quarters of a beat after the triad on the second 16th of beat 1, then the triad on the last 16th of beat 2 is three-quarters of a beat after the triad on beat 2, and so on. These three-quarters-of-a-beat increments are often found in 16th-note rock and funk rhythms. The left hand is playing the root (G) on beat 1 of each measure, followed by the fifth and root in a higher register, again in a rhythmic conversation with the right-hand part.

Straight-16ths Exercise #5

TRACK 13
0:00 56 bpm
0:24 83 bpm
0:41 110 bpm

This has a similar feel to the Straight-16ths Example #3, this time using more upper structure triad voicings:

- On the C#m7 in measure 1, the upper E major triad is built from the third.
- On the D/E in measure 1, the upper D major triad is built from the seventh. This slash chord is equivalent to an E9sus or E11 (suspended dominant) chord.
- On the E/A in measure 2, the upper E major triad is built from the fifth. This slash chord is equivalent to an Amaj9(omit3) or Amaj9(no3) chord.
- On the F#/G# in measure 2, the upper F# major triad is built from the seventh. This slash chord is equivalent to a G#9sus or G#11 (suspended dominant) chord.

The left hand is again playing the root of each chord in octaves.

Rhythmically, the left hand is playing the chord roots on beats 1 and 3, and the right hand is playing the upper triads on beats 2 and 4, all of which creates a strong foundation. The only 16th-note syncopation is around beat 3 in the right hand, which gives a sparse yet effective feel to this rhythmic groove.

Straight-16ths Exercise #6

TRACK 14
0:00 56 bpm
0:24 83 bpm
0:41 110 bpm

The last exercise in this chapter introduces some R&B/jazz voicings and rhythms for us to work with. Most of the voicings are either upper structure four-part shapes, or "seven-three extended," where we pick out the seventh and third of the chord, plus one extra note. These are all staple jazz voicing techniques, which we're now applying in a funky rock setting. Here's a look at the voicings in more detail:

- On the C9 (C dominant 9th) in measure 1, the upper Em7♭5 four-part chord is built from the third.

- On the F9 in measure 1, the upper Am7♭5 four-part chord is built from the third.

- On the B♭9 in measure 2, the upper Dm7♭5 four-part chord is built from the third.

- On the D7♯9 in measure 2, the right-hand shape is "seven-three extended": from bottom to top we have F♯ and C (the third and seventh), followed by F (the sharped ninth).

- On the G7♯5 in measure 2, the right-hand shape is "seven-three extended": from bottom to top we have F and B (the seventh and third), followed by E♭ (the sharped fifth).

- On the D♭9♯11 in measure 2, the upper B augmented triad is built from the seventh.

Meanwhile, the left hand is playing a melodic bass line part, moving between the chord roots using other chord tones (thirds and fifths) and half-step intervals.

Rhythmically, the right-hand voicings landing on the second 16th note in each beat give a heavily syncopated feel to this groove. This is further enhanced by the left hand, which anticipates (lands a 16th note ahead of) beat 3 in each measure. Have fun adding some jazz to your rock piano chops!

Further Reading

If you would like more information on some of the style and theory topics mentioned in this chapter, you may want to check out some of my other books, published by Hal Leonard Corporation.

For more information on using minor pentatonic scales, upper structure triads, and alternating triads in rock styles, check out *The Pop Piano Book* (HL00220011).

For more information on blues piano techniques, including the use of blues scales, drones, and Mixolydian modes, check out *Blues Piano: The Complete Guide with CD!* (HL 00311007).

For more information on jazz voicing techniques, including four-part and "seven-three extended" voicings, check out *Contemporary Jazz Piano: The Complete Guide with CD!* (HL00311848), and *Intro to Jazz Piano: The Complete Guide with CD!* (HL00312088).

Chapter 2
Rock Piano Groove Lab

The Groove Lab Concept

Now it's time to dig deeper into the rhythmic subdivision styles used in rock piano. Here we'll be working on rhythmic feel examples with straight- and swing eighths, and straight- and swing-16ths.

For each of these, we'll practice comping (accompanying) through a specific chord progression. We'll develop four different ways (from simpler to more complex) to comp over this progression, explaining the harmonic and rhythmic concepts being used at each stage. The CD tracks will have the left-hand part on the left channel and the right-hand part on the right channel, so you can isolate each hand's part as needed.

Then for each of the rhythmic feels, we'll have play-along Groove Lab tracks at four different tempos. These CD tracks have the rhythm section on the left channel and the piano part on the right channel. They are long enough for you to play all four comping variations twice each. You can also use these tracks to play extended repeats of any one of the comping variations, or to improvise your own comping grooves with the rhythm section!

Straight-eighths Groove Lab Exercises

Now we'll get to the first set of Groove Lab exercises, using the straight-eighths rhythmic feel. Again, the goal here is to develop your rock piano technique while also learning chord voicings and rhythms. Here's the chord progression we'll use for the straight-eighths exercises:

This is a common chord progression, used as a basis for many rock songs. Our first comping solution for this progression is as follows:

Straight-eighths Groove Variation #1

TRACK 15

9

Note that all the CD tracks for the individual Groove Variations in this chapter have the left-hand part on the left channel and the right-hand part on the right channel. The CD tracks for the straight-eighths Groove Variations are all recorded at 95 beats per minute.

This first variation is suitable for basic rock and heavy metal styles, with the root-fifth voicings in the right hand supported by the chord roots in the left. (Root-fifth voicings are often more suitable than triads, in the heavier rock styles.) Rhythmically, from measure 2 onward, the right hand is anticipating beat 1, i.e., landing on the "& of 4" and then tied over the barline. This anticipation gives the groove its energy and is commonly used in eighth-note rock styles. Meanwhile, the left hand anchors the groove by playing a dotted-quarter/eighth/half-note pattern, again typical for this style.

When playing through this groove, make sure the right-hand voicings anticipate the downbeats as described above, while the left hand still lands on the downbeats, i.e., the right hand plays ahead of the left hand. As with the Chapter 1 exercises, practice these grooves hands separately as needed before combining them. In particular, getting the left-hand patterns on autopilot is very helpful, as these tend to be repetitive in nature. On to the next Groove Variation for this progression:

Straight-eighths Groove Variation #2

TRACK 16

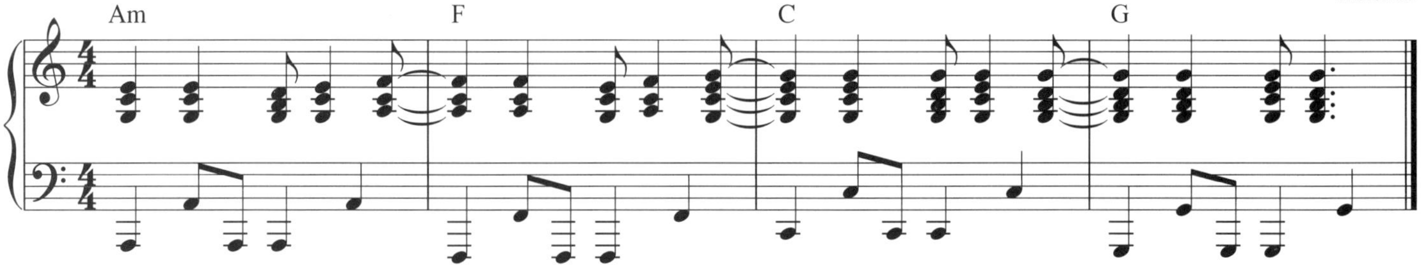

This second variation has more of a pop/rock feel, using "alternating triads" in the right hand. For example, over the Am chord in measure 1 we are moving between C and G major triads, then over the F major chord in measure 2 we are moving between F and C major triads, and so on. This adds some upper extensions to the basic chord symbols, and has a much more "pop" flavor when compared to Variation #1.

Rhythmically, the right hand is again anticipating beat 1 from measure 2 onward, and is also landing on the "& of 3," anticipating beat 4. The left-hand pattern is similar to variation #1, now with the root of each chord played by the thumb on beats 2 and 4 in the higher octave. These extra backbeats give forward motion to the groove.

Ensure that the right-hand triads are played legato (in a smooth and connected way) over the driving left-hand pattern. Make sure the right hand lands ahead of the left hand on the anticipations of beat 1.

Straight-eighths Groove Variation #3

TRACK 17

This third variation has a more open sound with the use of fourth and fifth intervals in the right hand, from the A minor pentatonic scale (A, C, D, E, and G). We first saw these "minor pentatonic fourths" used in Straight-eighths Exercise #3 in Chapter 1. We're also "targeting" certain chord tones with these intervals, either on beat 1 or its anticipation: the ninth and fifth on the F chord, and the root and fifth on the C and G chords.

Also, in measures 2 and 4 (on the "& of 3") we have a root-ninth-fifth-root voicing from bottom to top. On these voicings, you may find it easier to play the bottom two notes with the thumb of the right hand. The combination of the root, fifth, and ninth on these chords is very useful in more sophisticated modern rock styles.

Meanwhile, the left hand is driving the groove along, playing the root of each chord in a steady eighth-note pattern. When you play this example, make sure the left-hand part is very steady and consistent, and, as we have seen with other eighth-note left-hand parts, you may want to accent the downbeats a little more heavily—for that authentic rock feel!

Straight-eighths Groove Variation #4

TRACK 18

This fourth variation makes very effective use of "octave-doubled triads," triads with the top note doubled one octave lower, on each chord. Connecting lines are played between these triads, again using octaves. The left hand is supporting all this with basic root-fifth intervals and single root notes.

Rhythmically, the right-hand triads are landing on beat 1 of measures 1 and 3, and anticipating the chord changes going into measures 2 and 4. The left hand is playing a pattern similar to Straight-eighths Groove Variation #1, now with the fifth of the chord added. When you play this example, use the sustain pedal as indicated to blend the notes together within each chord.

Now it's time to combine these four Straight-eighths Groove Variations into one long Groove Lab example. The following CD tracks contain two repeats each of the preceding Groove Variations #1–#4, this time with a rhythm section on the left channel so you can play along with the band.

Straight-eighths Groove Variations #1–#4

TRACK 19 65 bpm   TRACK 20 85 bpm   TRACK 21 105 bpm   TRACK 22 125 bpm

Again, depending on your playing level, you can start at the slowest tempo CD track as needed, before moving on to the faster tempo tracks. Note that the rhythm section tracks on the left channel are the same for all four groove variations—just the piano part is different. This is a good illustration of some of the different choices you would have when comping through these changes with a band!

Here are some of the ways in which you can use these play-along tracks:

- Play through all the preceding four Groove Variations twice each (i.e., as written). Learning how to transition between these different rock comping styles is very beneficial.

- Choose just one of the Groove Variations, one that might be giving you problems, and play along with the rhythm track. The rhythm tracks are long enough for eight repeats of any one of the Groove Variations.

- Improvise your own rock comping parts on these changes, playing along with the rhythm section tracks.

Of course, you can mix and match these approaches as needed. Have fun!

The Swing-eighths Rhythmic Feel

Before we get to the next set of Groove Lab exercises, we need to understand the swing-eighths rhythmic feel used by a significant percentage of rock songs, especially blues/rock and classic rock.

In a swing-eighths feel, the second eighth note in each beat, the "&" in the rhythmic counting, lands two-thirds of the way through the beat. This is equivalent to playing on the first and third parts of an eighth-note triplet. We still count using "1 & 2 &," etc., but now each "&" is played a little later:

TRACK 23

Note that the first measure above looks the same as the straight-eighths example in Track 1, but when a swing-eighths interpretation is applied to it, it sounds equivalent to the second measure above, i.e., the quarter-eighth triplets. However, the second measure is more cumbersome to write and to read, so it is common practice to notate as in the first measure, but to interpret it in a swing-eighths style as needed.

Swing-eighths Groove Lab Exercises

On to the next set of Groove Lab exercises, now using the swing-eighths rhythmic feel. The CD tracks for the swing-eighths Groove Variations are all recorded at 90 beats per minute. Here's the chord progression we'll use for the swing-eighths exercises:

This would be a typical progression in pop/rock styles. Our first comping solution for this progression is as follows:

Swing-eighths Groove Variation #1

TRACK 24

This first variation uses basic triads in the right hand on all of the chords, except for the upper structure G major triad built from the third of the Em7 chord in measure 3, and the suspension (using the root, fourth, and fifth) on the Asus chord in measure 4. Also, the right hand is using a "split interval" technique at the end of measures 1 and 3: playing the outer notes of a triad followed by the inner (or middle) note. This is an effective embellishment technique in ballad and some rock styles. The left hand supports this by playing the chord roots in an octave pattern.

Rhythmically, the right-hand triads are landing on beat 1 and the "& of 2" (anticipating beat 3) in each measure, a common rhythmic figure in pop and rock styles. The left hand plays the lower note of the octave pattern on beats 1 and 3, with the upper note in each octave leading effectively into the backbeats (beats 2 and 4) being played by the right hand.

When playing this pattern, in the right hand, use the octave-doubled triad hand position needed for Straight-eighths Groove Variation #4. Even though no octaves are played in the right hand, this will result in far greater efficiency and smoothness of playing. For example, with the right-hand thumb on the A below middle C and the pinky on the A above middle C, you can play all the notes in measure 1 without moving your hand position. Similarly, with the right-hand thumb on the B below middle C and the pinky on the B above middle C, you can play all the notes in measure 2 without moving your hand position, and so on.

Note the triplet sign used over the A major triad arpeggio in the treble clef during measure 4. As we saw earlier, the swing-eighths subdivision uses the first and third parts of an eighth-note triplet. However, when we need to play on all three parts of the triplet, and in particular the middle part, the triplet sign is needed.

Swing-eighths Groove Variation #2

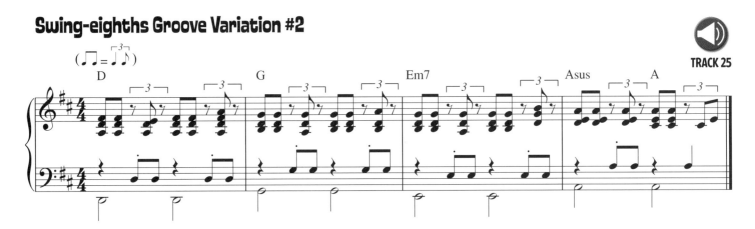

TRACK 25

This second variation adds some "resolutions" within the right-hand triads. For example, in measure 1 the note E moves to F♯ within the D major triad, and in measure 2 the note A moves to B within the G major triad. These are both examples of "9 to 3" or "2 to 3" movements within these triads. This is a staple embellishment technique across a range of pop and rock piano styles.

Rhythmically this is a busier pattern that uses all the eighth-note triplet subdivisions (between the hands) during beats 2 and 4 of each measure. For example, during beat 2 of measure 1, the left hand lands right on beat 2 (the first subdivision), then the right hand lands on the middle subdivision (therefore needing a triplet sign), and the left hand then lands on the last subdivision.

When playing this example, make sure the left-hand pinky holds down the root of each chord, while the thumb plays the rhythmic accents during beats 2 and 4, as described above. The right-hand accents during beats 2 and 4 should be kept fairly short, to accentuate the eighth-note triplet occuring between the hands.

Swing-eighths Groove Variation #3

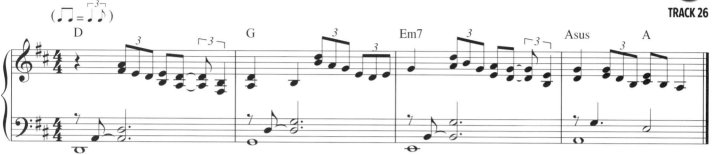

This third variation uses pentatonic scales in the right hand. In measure 1, all the third intervals, fourth intervals, and single notes come from the D pentatonic scale (D, E, F♯, A, and B). Similarly, all the notes in measure 2 come from the G pentatonic scale (G, A, B, D, and E). These scales are built from the root of each of these chords, which is an effective way to add a country flavor to your rock playing. The G pentatonic scale is also used in measure 3, built from the third of the Em7 chord, and in the first half of measure 4, built from the seventh of the implied A7sus chord, an upgraded version of the Asus chord symbol. Then in the second half of measure 4, the A pentatonic scale is used over the A major chord, again built from the root.

Meanwhile, the left hand is playing open arpeggio patterns: either root-fifth-root (on the D and G chords), root-fifth-third (on the Em7 chord), or root-seventh-fifth (on the Asus–A chords). The simpler left-hand rhythm is an effective support to the more melodic right-hand part. When practicing this pattern, play the right-hand pentatonic fills in a legato style and make sure they project over the left-hand arpeggios.

Swing-eighths Groove Variation #4

This fourth variation has an arpeggio-style right-hand part, which is a combination of basic and upper structure triad tones, and melodic/connecting tones from the major scale of the key signature (D major). For example, in measure 1, the first four notes in the right hand are A-D-F♯-A, an arpeggio of a D major triad. Then the top line moves from A to G to F♯ and so on, punctuated in between by the thumb playing A, the fifth of the chord. A similar combination of arpeggios and melody tones is used in measures 2 and 3, whereas in measure 4 we are using straight arpeggios on the Asus and A major chords. Below all this, the left hand is playing the roots in a simple octave pattern.

Rhythmically, the right hand is using all the available eighth-note triplet subdivisions. In this case, a notation alternative would be to use 12/8 time, where we would not need to write all the triplet signs. The choice between 4/4 and 12/8 notation is a matter of subjective preference—the music sounds the same either way, of course! Even if we notate in 4/4 time, we might still describe this pattern as having a 12/8 feel due to the use of all the subdivisions in the right hand. The left-hand quarter-note rhythms are a simple, effective support to the right-hand part.

Next we'll combine these four Swing-eighths Groove Variations into one long Groove Lab example. The following CD tracks contain two repeats each of the preceding Groove Variations #1–#4, again with the rhythm section on the left channel so you can play along with the band.

Swing-eighths Groove Variations #1–#4

As before, you can use these multiple-tempo play-along tracks to play through all the variations with repeats as written, or to focus on one of the variations for a longer time, or to improvise your own parts as desired.

Straight-16ths Groove Lab Exercises

Next up are the straight-16ths set of Groove Lab exercises. (Review Track 8 and accompanying text as needed, for information on the straight-16ths rhythmic subdivision.) The CD tracks for these Groove Variations are all recorded at 83 beats per minute. Here's the chord progression we'll use for the straight-16ths exercises:

The busier chord rhythms here, two chords per measure, are commonly used in the 16th-note rock and R&B/funk styles. Our first comping solution for this progression is as follows:

Straight-16ths Groove Variation #1

TRACK 32

This first variation uses a mix of basic and upper structure triads in the right hand. In measures 1–3, the E♭, A♭, and B♭ major triads are built from the thirds of the Cm7, Fm7, and Gm7 chords, respectively. Also, the C minor triad later in measure 3 is built from the third of the A♭maj7 chord.

The key rhythmic aspect of this groove is the right-hand triad landing on the last 16th of beat 2 (the "a of 2"), anticipating beat 3 by a 16th note. This is a staple piano device in R&B ballad and funk styles; it also works in the 16th-note rock styles. Meanwhile, the left-hand bass line is playing the chord roots on beats 1 and 3, with an eighth-note pickup into the following measure (on the "& of 4," halfway through beat 4).

When practicing this example, make sure your coordination is good around the beat 3 area, with the right hand anticipating the downbeat, and the left hand landing on the downbeat.

Straight-16ths Groove Variation #2

This second variation uses the same right-hand triads as the first, now within a busier rhythmic context. Inside beat 4 in each measure, there are some resolutions in the right-hand triads. For example, in measure 1 the C to D movement is a "9 to 3" within the B♭/D chord. The F on top is also the fifth of the chord. Similarly, in measure 2 the E♭ to F movement is a "7 to 1" inside the Fm7 chord. The A♭ on top is also the third of the chord, and so on. These two resolution phrases could also be derived from the B♭ and A♭ (equivalent to F minor) pentatonic scales, respectively.

Rhythmically, the right hand is still anticipating beat 3 by a 16th note, as in Groove Variation #1, and is now adding more 16th-note subdivisions, most importantly on the second 16th of beat 3 (the "e of 3") to intensify the syncopated effect. The left hand is now adding 16th-note pickups at the end of each measure, significantly adding to the forward motion of this groove.

When playing this example, keep the right-hand chords either side of beat 3 crisp and precise. The left-hand pickups at the end of each measure need to be played in a legato style into the following downbeats.

Straight-16ths Groove Variation #3

TRACK 34

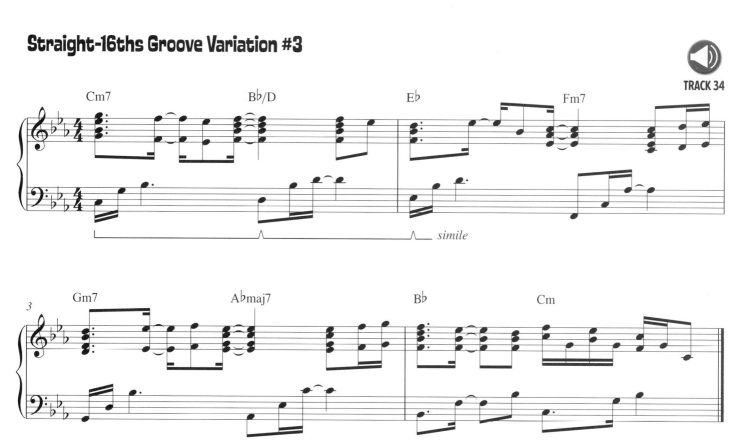

This third variation uses a mixture of triads (some octave-doubled), single-note octaves, suspensions, and fourth and fifth intervals in the right hand to create a bigger sound. The upper structure triad relationships are the same as in Variation #2, now in a higher register and with some octave doubling added. Connecting lines using octaves are played between these triads, adding more 16th-note anticipations.

In measure 4, the F-Bb-Eb on the last 16th of beat 1 is a suspension of the Bb chord. (I refer to this shape as a "double 4th," as it consists of one perfect fourth interval stacked on top of another). The fourth and fifth intervals and single notes on the Cm chord all come from the C minor pentatonic, or Eb pentatonic, scale, and are a good contrast to the preceding triad voicings.

The left hand is playing open arpeggios using various 16th-note rhythms. Note how, in measures 1–3, the left-hand arpeggio rhythms lead into the right-hand part. For example, in measure 1 on the Cm7 chord, the left-hand root-fifth-seventh arpeggio ends on the "& of 1," and the following right-hand octave lands immediately afterward on the last 16th of beat 1. Similarly, on the Bb/D chord, the left-hand third-root-third arpeggio ends on the last 16th of beat 3, and the following right-hand triad lands immediately afterward on beat 4. All this helps to build the energy of the pattern.

When you play this example, use the sustain pedal as indicated to blend the notes together within each chord, and play the 16th-note anticipations cleanly in the right-hand part.

Straight-16ths Groove Variation #4

TRACK 35

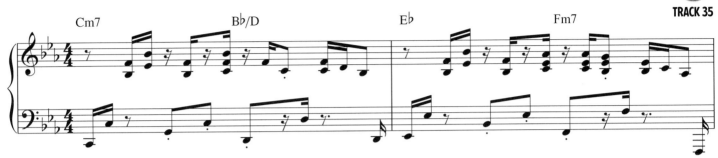

This fourth variation uses a mixture of fourth and fifth intervals, double 4ths, triads, suspensions, and pentatonic fills in the right hand, for a more sophisticated effect. At the beginning of measures 1 and 2, the B♭-F and E♭-B♭ fifth intervals collectively create the third, seventh, and fourth (11th) on the Cm7 chord, and the root, fifth, and ninth on the E♭ major chord. These modern, transparent sounds are good alternatives to triads. Later, in measure 1 on the B♭/D chord, we use the double 4th C-F-B♭, which is the ninth, fifth, and root of the B♭ chord, followed by a fill derived from the B♭ pentatonic scale. In measure 2 on the Fm7 chord, we are using the alternating upper triads A♭ and E♭, followed by a fill derived from the A♭ pentatonic, or F minor pentatonic, scale. During measures 3–4, the melodic top line over the chords, alternating between E♭ and D, is supported by a mix of triads, suspensions, and inverted double 4ths.

Rhythmically, this is the most intense 16th-note groove so far, with the right- and left-hand parts in an interlocking rhythmic conversation that uses most of the available subdivisions. The left-hand 16th-note octaves (at the beginning of measures 1–3, leading into the right-hand fifth intervals) effectively propel the groove. Note that the left hand is still anchoring the chord roots on beats 1 and 3 of each measure.

When practicing, you may find it helpful to isolate the right-hand part first, and then add the left-hand part, which is essentially added into the rhythmic spaces between the right-hand voicings. This is a good conceptual approach to building these funky 16-note rock comping parts.

Next we'll combine these four Straight-16ths Groove Variations into one long Groove Lab example. The following CD tracks contain two repeats each of the preceding Groove Variations #1–#4, with the rhythm section on the left channel so you can play along with the band.

Straight-16ths Groove Variations #1–#4

 TRACK 36 56 bpm   **TRACK 37** 74 bpm   **TRACK 38** 92 bpm   **TRACK 39** 110 bpm

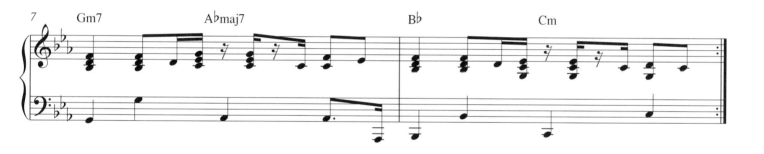

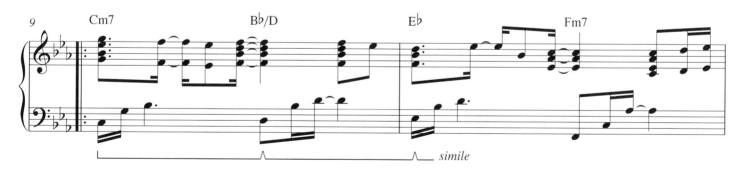

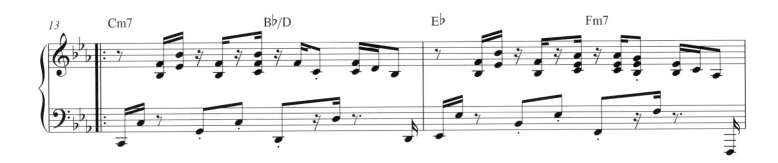

You can use these multiple-tempo play-along tracks to practice all the variations with repeats as written, or to focus on one of the variations for a longer time, or to improvise your own parts as desired.

The Swing-16ths Rhythmic Feel

Before we get to the last set of Groove Lab exercises, we need to understand the swing-16ths rhythmic feel. This is used extensively in modern funk and hip-hop styles, and is also found in some of the funkier and dance-oriented rock styles.

In a swing-16ths feel, the second and fourth 16th notes in each beat (the "e" and "a" in the rhythmic counting) land two-thirds of the way through each eighth note, rather than dividing it in half. This is equivalent to playing on the first and third parts of a 16th-note triplet. We still count using "1 e & a," etc., but now each "e" and "a" is played a little later:

TRACK 40

Note that the first measure above looks the same as the straight-16ths example in Track 8, but when a swing-16ths interpretation is applied to it, it sounds equivalent to the second measure above (i.e., the eighth-16th triplets). However, as the second measure is more cumbersome to write and to read, it is common practice to notate as in the first measure, but rhythmically to interpret in a swing-16ths style as needed.

Swing-16ths Groove Lab Exercises

On to the next set of Groove Lab exercises, now using the swing-16ths rhythmic feel. The CD tracks for the swing-16ths Groove Variations are recorded at 77 beats per minute. Here's the chord progression we'll use for the swing-16ths exercises:

This type of progression, using dominant chords, is commonly found in blues/rock styles, and adding the swing-16th subdivision would then give it a funkier sound. Our first comping solution for this progression is as follows:

Swing-16ths Groove Variation #1

TRACK 41

This first variation uses a lot of upper structure four-part chords in the right hand. All these are minor-seventh-with-flatted-fifth chords, built from the thirds of the dominant-seventh chord symbols and upgrading them to dominant-ninth chords overall. For example, in the first measure we have a G#m7b5 in the right hand, built from the third of the E7 chord. Similarly, in the second measure we have an F#m7b5 in the right hand, built from the third of the D7 chord, and so on. Note these upper four-part shapes are in second inversion. This gives a good balance and is often preferred. This voicing is a staple sound in blues/rock and classic fusion styles.

At the end of measure 4, the F# minor triad is a passing chord leading back to the E major triad. Technically, both these triads come from the E Mixolydian mode (containing the notes E, F#, G#, A, B, C#, and D), which is a basic scale source for the E7 chord.

Rhythmically, the right-hand voicings land on the second 16th of beat 1 (the "e of 1") in each measure, giving this groove a syncopated, funky effect. The right hand is also landing on all the backbeats (beats 2 and 4) in each measure. Meanwhile, the left-hand octave pattern is playing the low root at the point of chord change, with the thumb playing the root an octave higher, right before the backbeat being played by the right hand. All this is typical of the funkier rock and R&B keyboard styles.

When playing this groove, keep the 16th upbeats in the right hand short and precise, and make sure you delay the second and fourth 16th note in the beat, to get the swing-16th feel. Listen to the CD track as needed, to get comfortable with this rhythmic concept.

Swing-16ths Groove Variation #2

TRACK 42

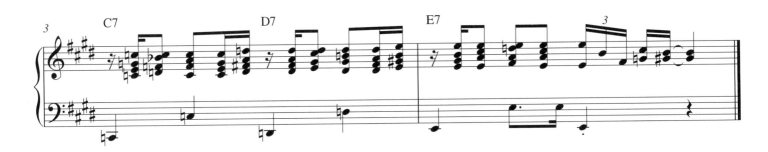

This second variation uses circle-of-fifths and circle-of-fourths movements in the right-hand triads. In my books and classes, I use the term circle-of-fifths to refer to a five-to-one harmonic relationship. For example, E is the fifth degree of A major, A is the fifth degree of D major, and so on. Similarly, I use the term circle-of-fourths to refer to a four-to-one harmonic relationship. For example, D is the fourth degree of A major, A is the fourth degree of E major, and so on.

Using this terminology, in measure 1 on the E7 chord, we have an E-A-D circle-of-fifths triad sequence, followed by a D-A-E circle-of-fourths triad sequence. Similarly, in measure 2 on the D7 chord, we have a D-G-C circle-of-fifths triad sequence, followed by a C-G-D circle-of-fourths triad sequence, and so on. This type of triad movement is borrowed from gospel and blues styles, and is sometimes referred to as "backcycling" in gospel circles.

For variation, we then have a bluesy fill in the right hand at the end of measure 4, with the ♭3rd moving to the third of the E7 chord (G to G♯) at the same time as the 13th moves to the fifth (C♯ to B)—a classic blues sound.

Rhythmically, this pattern is busier than Variation #1, with the right hand subdividing more during beats 1 and 3, and the left-hand roots landing on the downbeats. When playing this groove, practice the right hand as needed to get comfortable with the octave-doubled triads and octave hand position required. Make sure the "pinky" note (the top note E in measure 1, D in measure 2, etc.) projects cleanly.

Swing-16ths Groove Variation #3

This third variation uses triads derived from Mixolydian modes in the right hand, a favorite blues/rock piano technique for voicing dominant chords. We saw before that the E Mixolydian mode (containing the notes E, F♯, G♯, A, B, C♯, and D) is a scale source for the E7 chord. Just to review: the Mixolydian mode is derived by displacing a major scale to start on its fifth degree (i.e., displacing the A major scale to start on the note E creates E Mixolydian) or by taking a major scale and flatting the seventh degree (i.e., taking the E major scale and flatting the seventh degree creates E Mixolydian).

Looking at measure 1 on the E7 chord, all the triads in the right hand (Bm, A, G♯dim, F♯m, and E) belong to E Mixolydian, and to an A major scale. Similarly, in measure 2 on the D7 chord, all the triads in the right hand (Am, G, F♯dim, Em, and D) belong to D Mixolydian, and to a G major scale, and so on. Note that these Mixolydian triads are in second inversion, and the top notes of each phrase often start and end with basic chord tones of the dominant chord. For example, the first group of three triads on each dominant chord starts with the seventh of the chord on top (D in the case of the first E7 chord) and ends with the fifth of the chord on top (B in the case of the first E7 chord). This top note targeting is typical and gives a more musical and stylistic result.

After playing the root at the point of chord change, the left hand is then playing a more melodic line using the corresponding Mixolydian mode for each chord, in either a contrary or parallel motion with the right-hand part. This time the two hands are playing mostly concerted rhythms (same rhythm in both hands), except for some 16th-note pickups and downbeats in the left hand.

When playing this example, make sure the concerted rhythms are clean between the hands, and play the left-hand line in a legato (smooth and connected) style except where indicated.

Swing-16ths Groove Variation #4

TRACK 44

This fourth variation uses some "seven-three extended" voicings in the right hand. (We first used this type of voicing in Track 14.) These voicings use the seventh and third of the chord plus one other chord tone, the ninth in this case, and are particularly suited to dominant chords. For example, on the E7 chord in measure 1, the first right-hand voicing is G#-D-F#, which is the third, seventh, and ninth from bottom to top. Similarly, on the D7 chord in measure 1, the first right-hand voicing is F#-C-E, which is also the third, seventh, and ninth of the chord, and so on.

In the right hand, we're also using some half-step movements, giving us a bluesy and funky sound. During beats 1, 2, and 4 of measure 1, the right hand moves between the D and C# (seventh and 13th of the E7 chord, respectively). Also during beat 3, the right hand moves between the G and G# (♭3rd/#9th and third of the E7 chord, respectively). Similar half-step movements then occur on the subsequent dominant chords. These are classic funk and blues sounds being applied to this groove.

The left hand has returned to a sparser "rhythmically alternating" type of part, filling in the holes and adding some pickups into the right-hand phrases. Apart from the points of chord change, the left hand is playing mostly on 16th upbeats (weak 16ths), giving a syncopated feel to this groove.

When playing this example, make sure you play the right-hand half-step movements in a legato, connected way except where indicated. Also, the individual 16th notes in the left hand need to be short and precise, to be an effective rhythmic counterpoint to the right-hand part.

Finally in this chapter we'll combine these four Swing-16ths Groove Variations into one long Groove Lab example. The following CD tracks contain two repeats each of the preceding Groove Variations #1–#4, with the rhythm section on the left channel so you can play along with the band.

Swing-16ths Groove Variations #1–#4

Again, you can use these multiple-tempo play-along tracks to practice all the variations with repeats as written, or to focus on one of the variations for a longer time, or to improvise your own parts as desired.

Have fun playing along with the band on these Groove Lab tracks!

Further Reading

If you would like more information on some of the style and theory topics mentioned in this chapter, you may want to check out some of my other books.

For more information on resolutions within triads, pentatonic scale fills, R&B/funk rhythms, and double 4th chord voicings, check out *The Pop Piano Book* (HL00220011).

For more information on blues/rock piano techniques, including Mixolydian triads and blues fills, check out *Blues Piano: The Complete Guide with CD!* (HL00311007).

For more information on circle-of-fifths and circle-of-fourths theory concepts, check out *Contemporary Music Theory, Level One* (HL00220014) and *All About Music Theory* (HL00311468).

Chapter 3

Phrases and Licks Used by the Pros

In this chapter, we'll explore some piano phrases and licks that are based on on excerpts from famous rock songs. Each example is presented and explained, so that you'll be able to incorporate these ideas into your own playing as desired.

The CD tracks for the examples in this chapter have a rhythm section on the left channel and the piano part on the right channel, and are recorded at three different style-specific tempos. Most of the exercises are repeated twice at each tempo on the CD tracks. Depending on your playing level, you can start at the slowest tempo CD track as needed, before moving on to the faster tempo tracks.

"Speed of Sound" (Coldplay)

Our first example is based on an excerpt from "Speed of Sound" by Coldplay, which uses a straight-eighths rhythmic subdivision. This example starts with a pickup (incomplete) measure, and the right-hand part begins on beat 3 of this pickup measure. Be ready to start playing on the third beat of the count-off on the CD track.

TRACK 49
0:00 85 bpm
0:27 105 bpm
0:50 125 bpm

Here, the right-hand part is based on a melodic line alternating between D and E on top (played with the upper fingers) and A, G, and F♯ on the bottom (played with the thumb). These thumb notes are important target notes on the chords: the A is the root of the A major chord, the G is the third of the Em chord, and the F♯ is the third of the D major chord. All this gives a strong harmonic characteristic to the phrase. The left hand is playing a supportive role with either root-fifth or root-octave patterns.

This is a good example of the type of modal progression favored by Coldplay. (Their tune "Clocks" has a similar structure.) We hear A as the tonal center (key) of this example, yet the V (five) chord used in measure 2 is an E minor chord, rather than the E major chord we would expect in the key of A major. This is because the song is based on an A Mixolydian mode, including the note G, rather than an A major scale, which would include the note G♯. Observe the G natural signs occurring in the music, contradicting the G♯ in the key signature.

Rhythmically, the right-hand part lands on a lot of eighth-note upbeats, anticipating the downbeats, which adds forward motion to this example. When playing through this, make sure these eighth-note figures are clearly articulated, and use the sustain pedal as indicated to blend the notes together within each chord.

"Brick" (Ben Folds)

Next up is another straight-eighths example based on an excerpt from "Brick" by Ben Folds.

TRACK 50
0:00 85 bpm
0:22 105 bpm
0:40 125 bpm

In this example, the right-hand part is playing eighth-note arpeggios through the chord changes, repeating the top notes D and E in each measure. The lower notes in the right-hand part land on beat 1, the "& of 2," and beat 4, creating a melodic line that is reflected in the chord symbols. For example, in measure 1 the A lands on beat 1, which suspends the E7 chord (hence the E7sus chord symbol), then the G♯ lands on the "& of 2," which then resolves the chord to E7. Similarly, the movement between the F♯-G-A in measure 4 accounts for the chord symbols moving from D to Dsus and back to D. In the second measure, the A and E are the ninth and sixth of the G chord respectively, which is why the G6/9 chord symbol has been used.

The left hand is driving the groove along with a repeated eighth-note root pattern, typical of pop/rock styles. When playing this example, keep the left hand steady and consistent. You can accent the right-hand thumb notes to bring out the melodic line as desired.

"Ruby Baby" (Donald Fagen)

Our next example is based on an excerpt from the piano solo in "Ruby Baby" by Donald Fagen, the principal creative force behind the band Steely Dan. Whether working as a solo artist or with Steely Dan, Fagen has long been known for combining rock rhythms with blues and jazz harmonies. Although a fine keyboard player himself, Fagen often uses other keyboard players and session musicians on recordings. The solo in this case was recorded by the session great Greg Philinganes. This example uses a swing-eighths rhythmic subdivision, as follows:

TRACK 51
0:00 85 bpm
0:16 105 bpm
0:29 125 bpm

Here in the right hand we are using mainly the F Mixolydian mode, the basic scale source for the F7 chord, and the D blues scale, containing the notes D, F, G, A♭, A, and C. This is the "relative minor blues," built from the sixth degree, with respect to the key of F.

In measure 1, the first-inversion G minor and F major triads are from the F Mixolydian mode, giving this phrase a bit of a gospel flavor. In the second half of the measure, the single note line is from the D blues scale. Then in measure 2, the B♭–D interval comes from F Mixolydian, and might typically resolve down to A-C, except in this case the A♭ to A movement has been added, which is a ♭3rd-third resolution on the F7 chord. The A♭-C interval and the following notes A and C are all within the D blues scale outlined above.

Rhythmically, the pulse is being anchored by the left-hand root in octaves, landing on beat 1 and the "& of 2," anticipating beat 3. In the second measure, the same right-hand phrase occurs twice: first starting on beat 1, then on the "& of 2." This type of phrase repetition is called a "rhythmic displacement," and is a sophisticated sound heard in jazz and more advanced rock styles.

When you play this example, ensure that you swing the eighths and that the triplets are articulated cleanly. Refer to the CD track as needed.

"Good Thing" (Fine Young Cannibals)

Next up is swing-eighths example based on an excerpt from a piano solo in "Good Thing" by Fine Young Cannibals. The piano solo on the recording was played by Jools Holland, a great blues and boogie-woogie pianist who was also a member of the British rock band Squeeze. This example captures some of the great rock 'n' roll energy Holland is known for.

TRACK 52
0:00 95 bpm
0:24 115 bpm
0:45 135 bpm

In this example, the right-hand part in measures 1–3 is derived from the D blues scale, built from the tonic of the key (D minor). In measure 4, the right hand is playing octave-doubled triad versions of the A minor and G major chords. Meanwhile, the left hand is playing strong root-fifth quarter-note voicings throughout.

The right-hand blues scale phrases in measures 1 and 2 are typical of blues/rock and rock 'n' roll phrasing. In measure 1, we have a constantly repeating top note (drone) of D, and underneath we have the ♭5th to fifth (A♭ to A) movement within the scale. Then in measure 2 we have a crossover phrase, so called because the upper fingers of the right hand need to cross over the thumb in order to get to the lower notes of the phrase.

Rhythmically, the right hand is using all the available eighth-note triplet subdivisions in measures 1–2, giving this section a 12/8 feel. (See the text following Track 27.) By contrast, the right hand uses quarter-note triplets for the triads in measure 4. Listen to the CD as needed, to familiarize yourself with these different triplet subdivisions.

When you play this example, make sure that the top drone note D projects clearly in measure 1, and play the right-hand triplets as evenly as you can, especially at faster tempos.

"Statesboro Blues" (Chuck Leavell)

Our next example is based on an excerpt from Chuck Leavell's "Statesboro Blues." Chuck Leavell is one of the world's best-known blues and blues/rock pianists, and has peformed with many top bands, notably including the Allman Brothers and the Rolling Stones. This is another bluesy example, using a swing-eighths rhythmic subdivision.

TRACK 53
0:00 80 bpm
0:17 100 bpm
0:31 120 bpm

In this example, the right-hand part is almost entirely derived from the C Mixolydian mode (containing the notes C, D, E, F, G, A, and B♭), with the exception of the note D♯/E♭, which approaches the note E by half-step (creating a ♭3rd-third movement on the C7 chord). Some Mixolydian third intervals are used (E-G and F-A in measure 1, and G-B♭ and F-A in measure 2), as well as the fourth interval G-C in measure 2.

This is all supported in the left hand with a typical blues/rock figure, playing the root-fifth, root-sixth, and root-seventh intervals in a driving eighth-note rhythm. When playing this example, make sure the left-hand pattern swings the eighth notes and locks up correctly with the right hand for the eighth-note triplets in measure 2. (Check the CD track as needed.)

"Breathe" (James Blunt)

Next up is an example based on an excerpt from "Breathe" by James Blunt, which uses a straight-16ths rhythmic subdivision.

TRACK 54
0:00 70 bpm
0:20 85 bpm
0:36 100 bpm

In this example, the right hand is using basic triads as defined by the chord symbols, except for the D♭ major triad used over the B♭m chord toward the end of measure 1. This is an upper structure triad built from the third of the B♭m chord, briefly upgrading it to a B♭m7 chord overall. The left hand is alternating between the root and fifth of the chords in octaves, giving a solid foundation to the groove.

Rhythmically, this example has an interesting combination of eighth- and 16th-note rhythms. In fact, most of the pattern has a heavy eighth-note feel, with the right hand subdividing all the eighth notes during beats 1–3 of each measure. Then in the first measure, the right hand lands on the second and fourth 16ths of beat 4 (the "e" and "a" of 4), which contrasts with the preceding eighth notes to give a highly syncopated effect. In the second measure, both hands landing on the second 16th of beat 4 for the A♭ chord is a strong 16th upbeat or anticipation.

When playing this example, make sure the eighth-note triads are steady and even, and accentuate the above 16th-note syncopations as desired. Also, make sure that both hands lock up securely on the A♭ chord in measure 2.

"Lights" (Journey)

Our next example returns to a swing-eighths rhythmic feel, and is based on an excerpt from "Lights" by Journey, with Jonathan Cain on piano.

TRACK 55
0:00 60 bpm
0:23 75 bpm
0:41 90 bpm

This example repeats the note A in the right hand, mostly on the backbeats (beats 2 and 4) over the chord changes. Adding the note A to the B minor chord upgrades it to a B minor seventh, and adding A to the C major chord upgrades it to a C major sixth chord. Otherwise, the right hand is playing arpeggios (broken chords) using basic chord tones. The left hand is supporting this with simple root-and-fifth interval patterns.

In measure 2 in the right hand, we have a variation on beat 3: the notes E and A are played together, with E moving to F♯ (the third of the D major chord) right afterward. This all comes from the D pentatonic scale (containing the notes D, E, F♯, A, and B), which is built from the root of the D major chord, giving the pattern a country flavor.

Rhythmically, the right-hand arpeggios make use of all the available eighth-note triplet subdivisions, giving this example a 12/8 feel. When playing this groove, don't forget that the swing-eighths interpretation still applies in the left hand: the fifth of each chord lands two-thirds of the way through beats 1 and 3, rhythmically coinciding with the right-hand part.

"I Got the News" (Steely Dan)

Next up is an example is based on an excerpt from "I Got The News" by Steely Dan, which uses a straight-16ths rhythmic subdivision.

TRACK 56
0:00 80 bpm
0:17 100 bpm
0:31 120 bpm

As mentioned earlier, Steely Dan is noted for combining jazz harmony and melody with rock rhythms. On the recording of this song, the piano part was played by Victor Feldman, a noted jazz pianist and composer in the mid-to-late 20th century.

This example is based on extensions and alterations of a C7 dominant chord. The right hand repeats the sequence Bb-F#-G-F#. These notes are the seventh-#11th-fifth-#11th of the chord, respectively. Against this, the left hand repeats the parallel sequence Bb-Eb-E-Eb. These notes are the seventh- #9th-third-#9th of the chord, respectively. At the beginning of measure 1, the left-hand voicing contains the root, third, and seventh of the C7 chord. On beat 3 of measure 2, both hands combine to create a polychord voicing, containing the third, seventh, and #9th of the chord. Although this type of voicing is commonly used in jazz, it is not often heard in rock styles due to its sophisticated and altered-sound quality.

Rhythmically, this groove is also interesting and somewhat unusual. The rhythm section track on the left channel is playing a 16th-note funky rock groove, yet the piano part is superimposing eighth-note triplets over this groove. This would occur only in more sophisticated styles. When playing this example, concentrate on the downbeats, and subdividing the beat into three parts when playing. Don't get distracted by the 16th-note subdivisions in the rhythm track!

"Don't Let the Sun Go Down on Me" (Elton John)

Our next example is based on an excerpt from "Don't Let the Sun Go Down on Me" by Elton John, which uses a straight-16ths rhythmic subdivision at a ballad tempo.

TRACK 57
0:00 55 bpm
0:34 70 bpm
1:00 85 bpm

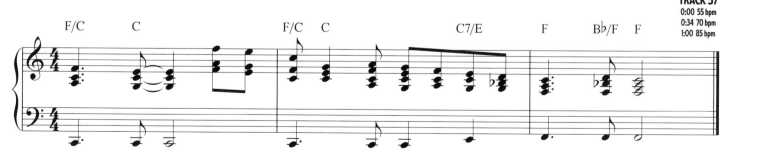

Elton John is a popular music icon who has long been known for infusing R&B and gospel influences into his pop/rock piano stylings. In measures 1 and 2, we have a "IV to I" movement into the C major chord (F/C to C), and in measure 3 we have a "I to IV and back to I" movement on the F major chord (F to B♭/F and back to F). These are typical gospel sounds, and use circle-of-fifths and circle-of-fourths triad movements in a way similar to the example in Track 42.

From measure 1 into measure 2, the right hand is using a filled-in octave technique, playing octaves with another note inside, a typical device in gospel as well as country and pop piano styles. Later in measure 2, full octave-doubled triads are used to create a denser effect.

The C major and G minor triads at the end of measure 2 collectively imply a C7 dominant chord, inverted over its third (E) in the bass register. This helps the progression lead strongly into the following F major chord.

Rhythmically, the left-hand root pattern is landing on beat 1, the "& of 2," and beat 3, a typical pop/rock and ballad rhythm. The right hand aligns with these rhythms in measures 2 and 3, and anticipates beat 3 in measure 1. When playing this example, make sure both hands lock up halfway through beat 2 in each measure, and be certain the right-hand octaves project cleanly in measures 1 and 2.

"Drops of Jupiter" (Train)

Our last example in this chapter is based on an excerpt from "Drops of Jupiter" by Train, with Brandon Bush on piano. This uses a swing-16ths rhythmic subdivision.

TRACK 58
0:00 70 bpm
0:33 85 bpm
1:01 100 bpm

This example uses a mix of alternating triads and fourth-interval-based voicings in the right hand, giving this groove a modern harmonic feel. In measure 1 on the C chord, we use a C major triad, followed by an F major triad as a passing chord during beat 4. In measure 2, we have a root-ninth-fifth voicing on the G chord (the notes G, A and D, from bottom to top). Technically, this is an inversion of the A-D-G double 4th shape. (See Track 35 for an earlier use of the double 4th voicing.) In this case, the double 4th shape is built from the ninth (A) of the chord. This is a staple sound in more modern and alternative rock styles. (See an earlier example in Track 17.)

Similarly, during beats 3 and 4 in measure 3, we have a root-ninth-fifth voicing on the F chord (the notes F, G and C, from bottom to top). This is an inverted double 4th, built from the ninth of the chord (G in this case). Elsewhere, we are moving between G and C major triads toward the end of measure 2 on the G chord, and between F major and D minor triads toward the end of measure 4 on the F chord.

Rhythmically, note that the only 16th-note syncopation we are playing is on the second 16th of beat 4 (the "e of 4") in each measure. This gives a sparse, funky feel to this groove. When practicing the example, make sure you are playing this syncopation accurately. The rhythm section track is outlining the swing-16th subdivisions, so that should help you line up the rhythm correctly.

Further Reading

If you would like more information on some of the style and theory topics mentioned in this chapter, you may want to check out some of my other books.

For more information on filled-in octaves, backcycling, and other gospel piano techniques, check out *The Pop Piano Book* (HL00220011).

For more information on blues piano drone and crossover phrases, check out *Blues Piano: The Complete Guide with CD!* (HL00311007).

For more information on modal chord progressions, check out *All About Music Theory* (HL00311468).

For more information on dominant chord extensions and alterations, check out *Contemporary Music Theory, Level Three* (HL00290538).

Chapter 4
Rock Piano Etudes

In this chapter, we have five etudes written in the style of famous rock pianists. Playing these along with the rhythm section on the CD is a great way to develop your rock piano chops! These etudes include both comping (accompaniment) and soloing/improvisational parts, and will help you get inside the playing styles of today's top performers.

As we work through each tune, we'll label the different sections: for example, Intro, A section or Verse, B section or Chorus, C Section or Bridge, Solo, Coda or end section, and so on. In this chapter, we will use the labels A, B, and C (also known as "rehearsal letters"), because we are focusing on the instrumental parts. However, as rock music is a vocal-oriented style, be aware that labels such as Verse, Chorus, and Bridge are also commonly used.

On the CD tracks, the band (minus the piano) is on the left channel, and the piano is on the right channel. In addition to bass and drums, other instruments such as organ and synthesizers have been added to flesh out the arrangements. Slow and Full Speed tracks are provided on the CD for each song.

Etude #1: Westbound Road

Our first etude is a straight-eighths pop/rock example in the key of D major. In the first A section (labeled A1), the piano part begins with right-hand triad voicings, with some arpeggios and pentatonic fills. Here, as in other sections, the right hand often lands halfway through beat 2, anticipating beat 3, a signature rhythmic figure in eighth-note rock styles. All this is supported by the left hand playing the root in an octave pattern.

This rhythmic feel continues into the first B section, now adding some inverted double 4th voicings and sixth intervals in the right hand. This then leads into the first C section, with the right hand playing octave-doubled triads in the higher register, connected melodically by single-note or filled-in octave lines. In the left hand, open arpeggio patterns are now added, to broaden the sound and to add harmonic definition.

In the second A section, both hands are playing in an arpeggio style, with accents on beat 1, the "& of 2," and beat 4. Although all the eighth-note subdivisions are used, this section sounds like an interlude and has a less intense feel. This transitions into the second C section, now with 16th-note arpeggios in the right hand, supported by solid root-fifth intervals in the left hand.

Finally, the Coda section is a reworked version of the A section chord changes, again with octaves and octave-doubled triads in the right hand, supported by open arpeggios in the left hand.

When playing this etude, ensure that the right-hand octaves are cleanly projected in the C1 and Coda sections, and play the 16th-note arpeggios as evenly as you can in the C2 section. Rock on!

TRACK 59
slow:
85 bpm

TRACK 60
full speed:
122 bpm

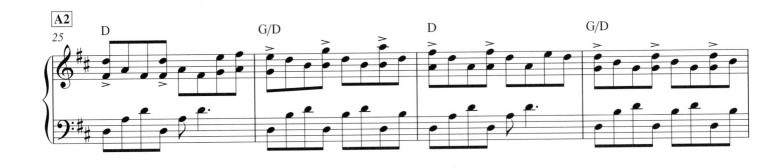

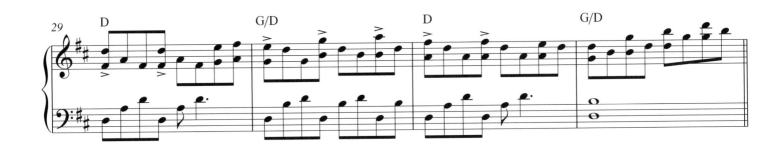

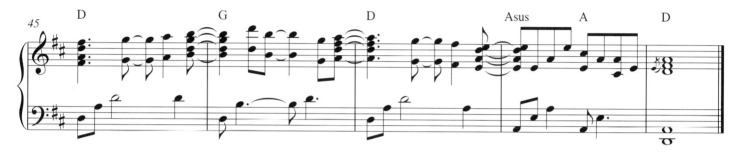

Etude #2: Chuck's Groove

The next etude is a more up-tempo straight-eights rock example, this time in the key of C major. The Intro section sets things up with a right-hand triad figure using eighth-note upbeats, creating a syncopated effect against the left-hand thumb playing on beats 2 and 4. Then the first and second A sections use right-hand drones (repeated top notes) over melody lines, as well as pentatonic scale and Mixolydian mode fills. These devices add country and blues flavors to this rock groove.

In the first and second B sections, the right hand plays a piano solo based on the B♭ and C pentatonic scales, supported by root-fifth and triad voicings in the left hand. Toward the end of the second B section, this solo transitions into an F pentatonic scale figure over the F/G chord. This leads into the Coda section, based on the Intro, but with a unison pentatonic scale figure added for the final ending.

Make sure you keep the right-hand anticipations tight and precise in the Intro and Coda sections, and bring out the right-hand drone (top) notes in the A sections. When you're ready, experiment with your own right-hand solo ideas over the changes in the first and second B sections!

TRACK 61
slow:
120 bpm

TRACK 62
full speed:
170 bpm

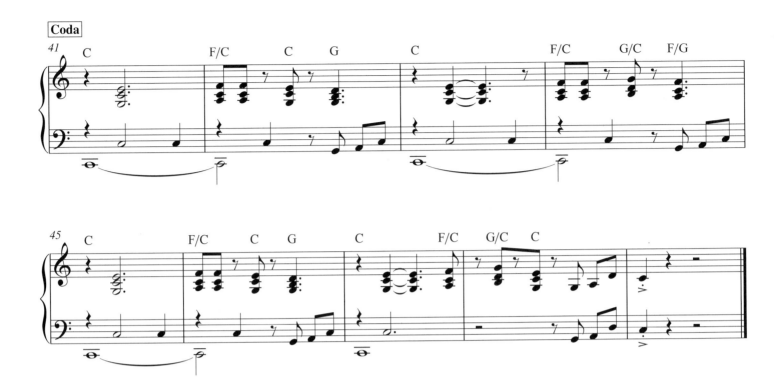

Etude #3: Streetlight People

Next we have an etude in a medium straight-eighths pop/rock style. In the first and second A sections there is something of a reversal of roles occurring rhythmically between the hands. In pop/rock piano styles, the right hand often anticipates the left hand, with the right-hand voicing landing an eighth note ahead of the beat, and the left hand landing on the beat, as seen in various examples in this book. In this case, however, the left-hand bass line is often anticipating beat 1, whereas the alternating eighth-note figure in the right hand always lands on beat 1. This is a bit unusual and may take some getting used to. You can practice these parts hands separately at first, if needed.

Here in the right-hand part, the note B is a common tone (pedal point) across all the changes, and combines with either F♯ or E underneath to create a series of fourth and fifth intervals on all the downbeats. All this makes for a modern, transparent sound.

In the first and second B sections, we switch to alternating triads in the right-hand part (moving between two different triads over the same bass note), adding octaves and filled-in octaves to invent fills at the end of the four-measure sections. These right-hand devices are underpinned by a steady eighth-note root pattern that drives the groove along. This is all typical of classic pop/rock keyboard styles.

Finally, the Coda section is essentially a repeat of the earlier A section, leading to a simple root-fifth voicing on the final B major chord. When playing this example, make sure your rhythmic coordination in the A sections is accurate (as discussed above), and in the B sections play the left-hand pattern in a steady and consistent way, accenting the downbeats a little if desired.

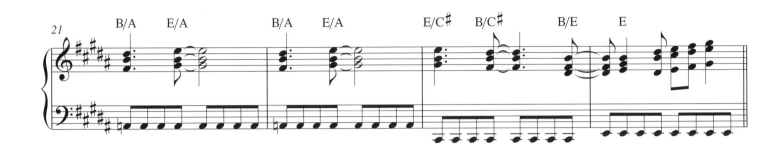

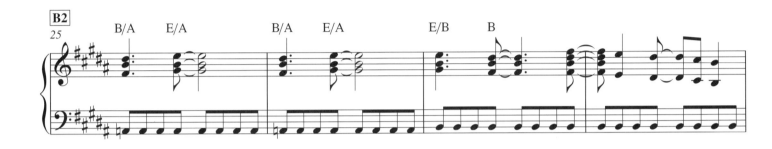

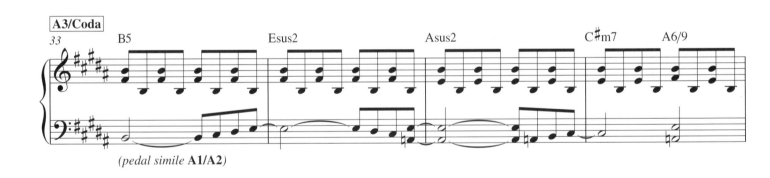

(pedal simile A1/A2)

Etude #4: Any Open Door

The next etude is a straight-16ths rock example in the key of B major, and contains many great piano techniques used by rock pianists—pentatonic fills and runs, double 4th voicings and arpeggios, and 16th-note octave syncopations.

The first A section gets things going with right-hand upper-structure triad voicings, interspersed with added ninths, pentatonic scale fills, and arpeggios of double 4th shapes. (For example, the fill in measures 4 and 8 is based on the double 4th F♯-B-E, built from the ninth of the Eadd9 chord.) The rhythmic figure then changes going into the second A section, with the voicings landing on the "& of 2" and also on beat 3, instead of anticipating beat 3, as in the first A section. Here, we have a busier feel, especially from measure 13 onward, with the right-hand 16th-note octave anticipations.

Starting in measure 17, we have the piano solo section. This is all classic rock piano stuff, such as arpeggios of double 4ths (measures 17, 19, 21, etc.), pentatonic scale runs and fills (measures 18, 20, 23, etc.), drone-note phrases (measures 27–28) and so on. This is supported in the left hand by a mix of root-fifth and root-seventh voicings, and open-triad arpeggios later in the solo. Finally, the Coda section is a repeat of the second A section, ending on the upper structure triad voicing B/E.

When playing this example, make sure the right-hand 16th-note octave rhythms are precise in the last half of the A2 and Coda sections. When you're ready, have fun adding your own pentatonic and double 4th-style fills and solo ideas as you play along with the backing track!

TRACK 65
slow:
75 bpm

TRACK 66
full speed:
108 bpm

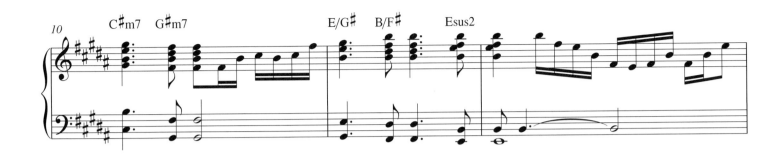

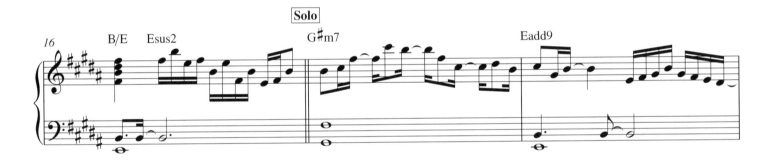

Etude #5: Prophets and Angels

Our last etude is a swing-eighths gospel/rock example in the key of F major. Rhythmically, this example often uses all the eighth-note triplet subdivisions within the beat, as seen from the triplet signs in the music. We noted earlier that this typically results in a 12/8 feel, and indeed using a 12/8 time signature would have been a notation alternative for this example. Also, some or all the eighth notes within a triplet are sometimes further subdivided in half (i.e., into 16th notes), hence the "6" or sextuplet signs in the music. Don't forget to check the CD track to get comfortable with these rhythms. You'll probably find that they sound easier than they look at first glance.

In the Intro section, the piano part begins with staple gospel-piano devices in the right hand: the I-IV-I triad movement on the F major chord in measure 1 (also known as backcycling), the eighth-note triplet octave runs during beats 2 and/ or 4, and the grace notes moving from the ♭3rd to the third of the F and C7 chords. The left hand supports all this with an octave-root note pattern, generally with the thumb landing on the "& of 2," anticipating beat 3. Then the first A section builds further, with more octave-doubled triads, eighth-note triplet subdivisions, and 16th-note arpeggios and fills. The triads inverted over their thirds in the bass (i.e., the B♭/D and C/E chords in measure 8) are supported with open-triad arpeggios in the left hand, a device borrowed from pop ballad styles.

The B section starts with a busier chord rhythm, four chords per measure, but has a more relaxed, less intense feel. However, this section builds up with chordal syncopations in measures 19–20, leading into the second A section. This is a busier, more intense version of the first A section, with the right hand using passing chords, arpeggios, and octave fills—all typical of gospel piano styles. Finally, the Coda section is based on the Intro, but with further rhythmic subdivisions and passing chords.

When playing this example, make sure the right-hand octave fills really project, and play the tuplet figures accurately, as noted earlier. Have fun with this very uplifting slice of gospel/rock!

TRACK 67
slow:
40 bpm

TRACK 68
full speed:
55 bpm

Appendix

Major Scales

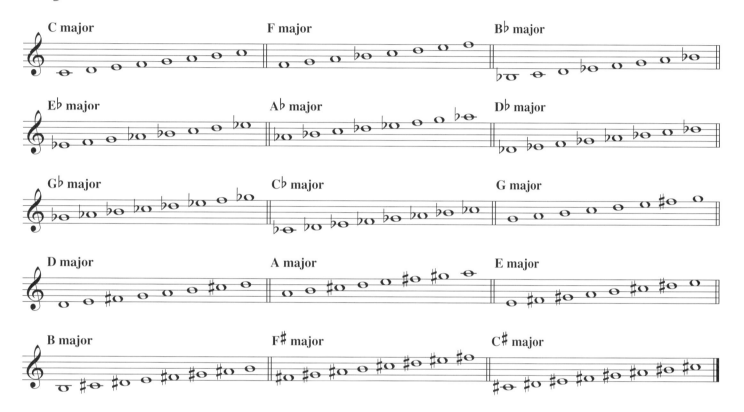

Key Signatures

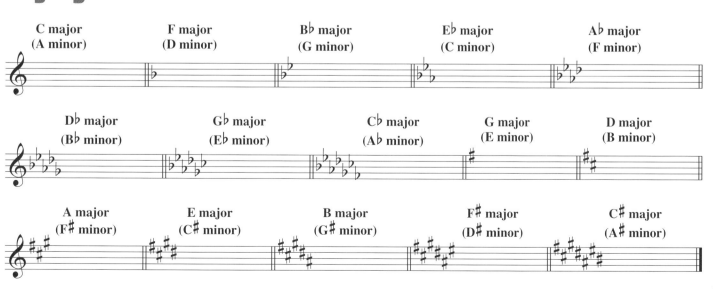

Mixolydian Modes

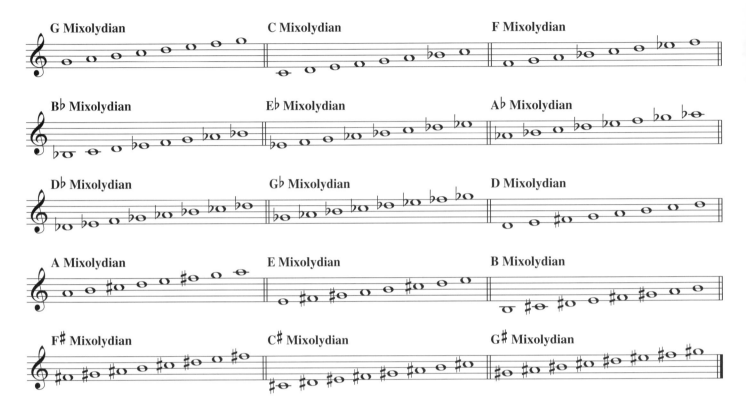

Pentatonic Scales

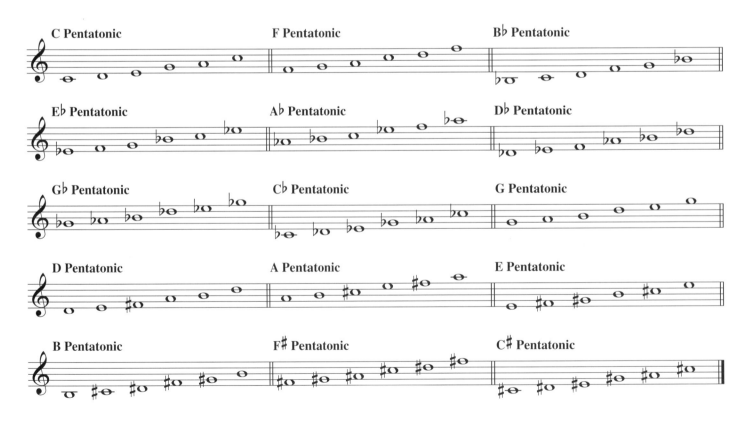

Minor Pentatonic Scales

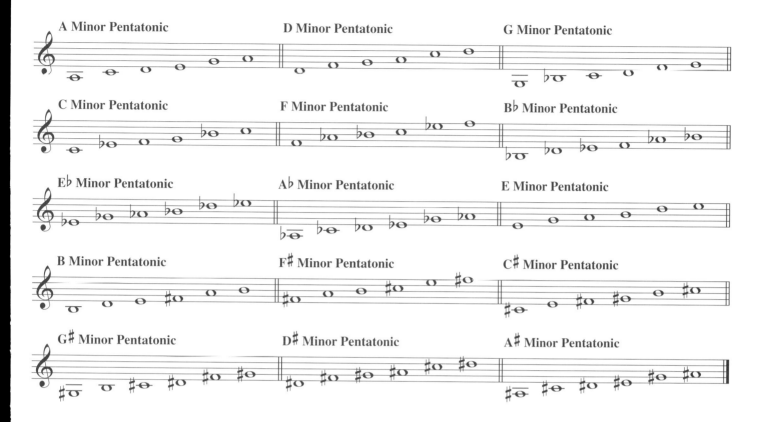

Blues Scales

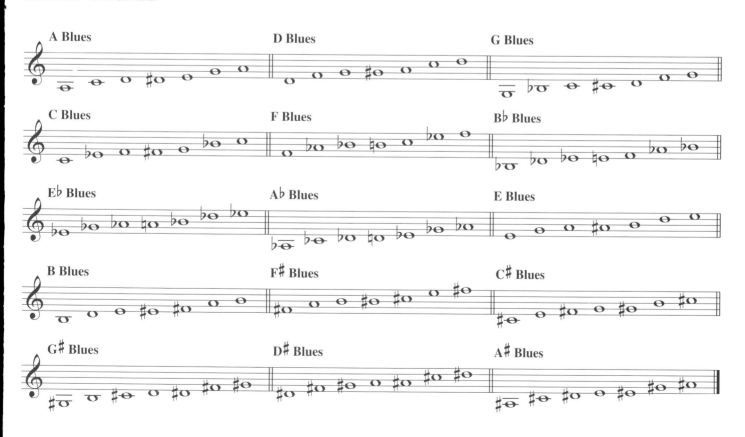

About the Author

Mark Harrison is a professional keyboardist, composer/arranger, and music educator/author based in Los Angeles. He has worked with top musicians such as Jay Graydon (Steely Dan), John Molo (Bruce Hornsby band), Jimmy Haslip (Yellowjackets), and numerous others. Mark currently performs with his own contemporary jazz band (the Mark Harrison Quintet) as well as with the Steely Dan tribute band Doctor Wu. His TV music credits include *Saturday Night Live*, *The Montel Williams Show*, *American Justice*, *Celebrity Profiles*, *America's Most Wanted*, *True Hollywood Stories*, the British documentary program *Panorama*, and many others.

Mark taught at the renowned Grove School of Music for six years, instructing hundreds of musicians from all around the world. He currently runs a busy private teaching studio, catering to the needs of professional and aspiring musicians alike. His students include Grammy winners, hit songwriters, members of the Boston Pops and L.A. Philharmonic orchestras, and first-call touring musicians with major acts.

Mark's music instruction books are used by thousands of musicians in over 20 countries, and are recommended by the Berklee College of Music for all their new students. He has also written Master Class articles for *Keyboard* and *How to Jam* magazines, covering a variety of different keyboard styles and topics. For further information on Mark's musical activities, education products, and online lessons, please visit *www.harrisonmusic.com*.

KEYBOARD STYLE SERIES

THE COMPLETE GUIDE WITH CD!

These book/CD packs provide focused lessons that contain valuable how-to insight, essential playing tips, and beneficial information for all players. From comping to soloing, comprehensive treatment is given to each subject. The companion CD features many of the examples in the book performed either solo or with a full band.

BEBOP JAZZ PIANO
by John Valerio

This book provides detailed information for bebop and jazz keyboardists on: chords and voicings, harmony and chord progressions, scales and tonality, common melodic figures and patterns, comping, characteristic tunes, the styles of Bud Powell and Thelonious Monk, and more. Includes 5 combo performances at the end of the book.

00290535 Book/CD Pack...$18.95

BEGINNING ROCK KEYBOARD
by Mark Harrison

This comprehensive book/CD package will teach you the basic skills needed to play beginning rock keyboard. From comping to soloing, you'll learn the theory, the tools, and the techniques used by the pros. The accompanying CD demonstrates most of the music examples in the book.

00311922 Book/CD Pack...$14.99

BLUES PIANO
by Mark Harrison

With this book/CD pack, you'll learn the theory, the tools, and even the tricks that the pros use to play the blues. You also get seven complete tunes to jam with on the CD. Covers: scales and chords; left-hand patterns; walking bass; endings and turnarounds; right-hand techniques; how to solo with blues scales; crossover licks; and more.

00311007 Book/CD Pack...$17.95

BRAZILIAN PIANO
by Robert Willey and Alfredo Cardim

Brazilian Piano teaches elements of some of the most appealing Brazilian musical styles: choro, samba, and bossa nova. It starts with rhythmic training to develop the fundamental groove of Brazilian music. Next, examples build up a rhythmic and harmonic vocabulary that can be used when playing the original songs that follow.

00311469 Book/CD Pack...$19.99

CONTEMPORARY JAZZ PIANO
by Mark Harrison

From comping to soloing, you'll learn the theory, the tools, and the techniques used by the pros. The full band tracks on the CD feature the rhythm section on the left channel and the piano on the right channel, so that you can play along with the band.

00311848 Book/CD Pack...$17.99

COUNTRY PIANO
by Mark Harrison

Learn the theory, the tools, and the tricks used by the pros to get that authentic country sound. This book/CD pack covers: scales and chords, walkup and walkdown patterns, comping in traditional and modern country, Nashville "fretted piano" techniques and more. At the end, you'll get to jam along with seven complete tunes.

00311052 Book/CD Pack...$17.95

GOSPEL PIANO
by Kurt Cowling

This comprehensive book/CD pack provides you with the tools you need to play in a variety of authentic gospel styles, through a study of rhythmic devices, grooves, melodic and harmonic techniques, and formal design. The accompanying CD features over 90 tracks, including piano examples as well as the full gospel band.

00311327 Book/CD Pack...$17.95

INTRO TO JAZZ PIANO
by Mark Harrison

This comprehensive book/CD is the perfect *Intro to Jazz Piano*. From comping to soloing, you'll learn the theory, the tools, and the techniques used by the pros. The accompanying CD demonstrates most of the music examples in the book. The full band tracks feature the rhythm section on the left channel and the piano on the right channel, so that you can play along with the band.

00312088 Book/CD Pack...$14.99

JAZZ-BLUES PIANO
by Mark Harrison

This comprehensive book will teach you the basic skills needed to play jazz-blues piano. Topics covered include: scales and chords • harmony and voicings • progressions and comping • melodies and soloing • characteristic stylings.

00311243 Book/CD Pack...$17.95

JAZZ-ROCK KEYBOARD
by T. Lavitz

Learn what goes into mixing the power and drive of rock music with the artistic elements of jazz improvisation in this comprehensive book and CD package. This instructional tool delves into scales and modes, and how they can be used with various chord progressions to develop the best in soloing chops.

00290536 Book/CD Pack...$17.95

LATIN JAZZ PIANO
by John Valerio

This book is divided into three sections. The first covers Afro-Cuban (Afro-Caribbean) jazz, the second section deals with Brazilian influenced jazz – Bossa Nova and Samba, and the third contains lead sheets of the tunes and instructions for the play-along CD.

00311345 Book/CD Pack...$17.99

POST-BOP JAZZ PIANO
by John Valerio

This book/CD pack will teach you the basic skills needed to play post-bop jazz piano. Learn the theory, the tools, and the tricks used by the pros to play in the style of Bill Evans, Thelonious Monk, Herbie Hancock, McCoy Tyner, Chick Corea and others. Topics covered include: chord voicings, scales and tonality, modality, and more.

00311005 Book/CD Pack...$17.95

PROGRESSIVE ROCK KEYBOARD
by Dan Maske

From the classic sounds of the '70s to modern progressive stylings, this book/CD provides you with the theory and technique to play and compose in a multitude of prog rock styles. You'll learn how soloing techniques, form, rhythmic and metrical devices, harmony, and counterpoint all come together to make this style of rock the unique and exciting genre it is.

00311307 Book/CD Pack...$17.95

Prices, contents, and availability subject to change without notice.

Visit Hal Leonard online at
www.halleonard.com

FOR MORE INFORMATION, SEE YOUR LOCAL MUSIC DEALER, OR WRITE TO:

HAL•LEONARD®
CORPORATION

7777 W. BLUEMOUND RD. P.O. BOX 13819 MILWAUKEE, WI 53213

R&B KEYBOARD
by Mark Harrison

From soul to funk to disco to pop, you'll learn the theory, the tools, and the tricks used by the pros with this book/CD pack. Topics covered include: scales and chords, harmony and voicings, progressions and comping, rhythmic concepts, characteristic stylings, the development of R&B, and more! Includes seven songs.

00310881 Book/CD Pack...$17.95

ROCK KEYBOARD
by Scott Miller

Learn to comp or solo in any of your favorite rock styles. Listen to the CD to hear your parts fit in with the total groove of the band. Includes 99 tracks! Covers: classic rock, pop/rock, blues rock, Southern rock, hard rock, progressive rock, alternative rock and heavy metal.

00310823 Book/CD Pack...$17.95

ROCK 'N' ROLL PIANO
by Andy Vinter

Take your place alongside Fats Domino, Jerry Lee Lewis, Little Richard, and other legendary players of the '50s and '60s! This book/CD pack covers: left-hand patterns; basic rock 'n' roll progressions; right-hand techniques; straight eighths vs. swing eighths; glisses, crushed notes, rolls, note clusters and more. Includes six complete tunes.

00310912 Book/CD Pack...$17.95

SALSA PIANO
by Hector Martignon

From traditional Cuban music to the more modern Puerto Rican and New York styles, you'll learn the all-important rhythmic patterns of salsa and how to apply them to the piano. The book provides historical, geographical and cultural background info, and the 50+-track CD includes piano examples and a full salsa band percussion section.

00311049 Book/CD Pack...$17.95

SMOOTH JAZZ PIANO
by Mark Harrison

Learn the skills you need to play smooth jazz piano – the theory, the tools, and the tricks used by the pros. Topics covered include: scales and chords; harmony and voicings; progressions and comping; rhythmic concepts; melodies and soloing; characteristic stylings; discussions on jazz evolution.

00311095 Book/CD Pack...$17.95

STRIDE & SWING PIANO
by John Valerio

Learn the styles of the stride and swing piano masters, such as Scott Joplin, Jimmy Yancey, Pete Johnson, Jelly Roll Morton, James P. Johnson, Fats Waller, Teddy Wilson, and Art Tatum. This book/CD pack covers classic ragtime, early blues and boogie woogie, New Orleans jazz and more. Includes 14 songs.

00310882 Book/CD Pack...$17.95